BROKEN ALBION

BY

HARRY WHITEWOLF

CONTENTS

Get Boris Done

Our Prime Minister is a big fat Johnson,

And his Brexit will be just as hard.

***

Broken Albion

Broken Albion

Becomes blue-bruised.

We've chlorinated chickened out,

And now we've cooked our goose.

Albion dragoons

Think they serve a civil war,

But they fight so uncivilly,

And they know not what they fight for.

Albion baboons

Beat their white British breasts.

Hear the drum: Get Brexit done.

And forget about the rest.

Albion traitors

Pretend they're patriots.

Glad gladiators,

Road-raging in chariots.

Albion's green is going,

Albion's waters are rising,

Whilst Boris beckons the furthest right

To be knights of the new uprising.

And all the Scots will leave.

And don't forget the Taffies.

Segregated. Against each other.

We're nothing but political patsies.

Albion is broken,

But rich plans stay in place.

Milk and manipulate us,

For Albion's disgrace.

***

Don't Pigeonhole Me, You Bastards

I'm not a remainer.

I'm not a leaver.

It's a no-brainer.

I'm a believer

In everything our political system isn't.

***

I Guess I'm a Remainer,
But It's Not as Simple as That

I guess I'm a remainer,

'Cos I think it's a *huge* mistake,

For us to leave the EU,

To put jobs at stake,

And end free movement,

And change protective laws,

And be less welcome to immigrants,

And put borders off our shores,

But that doesn't mean

I don't still think,

The EU's full of twats

Making decisions that stink.

***

We're Only Making Plans for Nigel

We have been done up like a right Ukipper,

'Cos the Brexit boat sailed without a skipper.

We cast our votes based on Farage's lies;

European marriages we must despise.

It's scary to think how just one bigoted man

Was the cause of the referendum; with a hand

From the BBC giving UKIP air time.

Have never seen that for the Green Party's kind.

The Brexit boat's route was never planned.

The Brexit boat's crew's been left unmanned.

We have been done up like a far right Ukipper,

Because the Brexit boat never had a skipper.

***

"We Knew What
We Were Voting For!"

13

"People didn't know what they were voting for."

"We knew what we were voting for!"

"People didn't know what they were voting for."

"We knew what we were voting for!"

Um, excuse me,

But you can't possibly

Know what 17,410,742 people were voting for,

So please replace the plural pronoun with a personal

pronoun in your regurgitated statement.

***

You Can Count on the Cunts

You can count on the cunts

To keep you down.

You can count on more cuts

And buckets of sand

To put on your heads,

As health and art dies.

You can count on the cunts

To bleed us all dry.

You can count on warmongers

To find budgets for arms.

You can count on Big Pharma

To sedate us with harm.

You can count on MPs

To keep up their lies.

You can count on fat cats

To treat us like mice.

You can count on greed

And selfishness.

You can count on injustice

And the helpless mess.

You can count on two fingers

Their secret rules of thumb.

Yeah, you can count on the powerful

To be a bunch of cunts.

***

The Wage Age

It's a shilling for shit

And a tuppenny for toss.

Spend all your money

On bollocks and dross.

Spend all your profits

On whiskey and dope.

'Cos it's a sixpence for lies

And a ha'penny for hope.

***

The Angry Bar

There's an angry bar

Down in Shangri La,

Where the champagne's spiked with spit.

And the caviar

Appears fancier

Because it's garnished with shit.

Best avoid dessert

'Cos it's made of dirt,

And blood, sweat, toil and sins.

The cook's gone berserk.

He does nowt but work.

Now there's arsenic in the mints.

***

Headline Mentality

It's time for some reflection,

'Cos there's a common misconception

That the Tories stand for Leave and Labour stand for

Remain,

And that's the reason why 2019 saw Brexit become so

delayed.

But it's bullshit, as you should well know.

Didn't you see members of both parties, and both

leavers and remainers, leaving their parties and getting

fired from their parties because they didn't agree with

the deal?

Wasn't Theresa May a remainer?

Every vote to get Brexit through wasn't thwarted

because of remainers,

But because of politicians on *both sides* wanting a

better deal...

It had nothing to do with *stopping* Brexit.

The shambles happened because they couldn't agree on

a deal.

Then the general election came,

And people believed it was as simple as:

Red = Remain (but won't admit it) and Blue = Leave.

***

At Least Everyone Agreed on One Thing

You lose some, you win some,

But if you're Jo Swinson,

You only lose.

***

Remoaner Stereotyping
Just Ain't True

The fact that

Nobody backed

The Lib Dem tact

Of stopping Brexit is proof that

Many remainers don't want to stop it,

Because it would be undemocratic,

No matter how much they believe Brexit's wank.

***

He's Just a Stereotype...

"All these remainers are all the same."

Sure. And all leavers are Union-Jack-flag-waving, anti-immigration-believing, white-supremacist, Muslim-hating, royalist, football-hooligan, semolina, bangers-and-mash, and steak-and-kidney-pie-eating racists.

When will people get it into their heads that stereotypes aren't true?

***

Get Brexit Done:
You Have Been Done

All you've got to do is reach stalemate,

And make the public so fatigued,

That they're willing to do anything;

Like give their votes to fat cat greed.

The people didn't vote Conservative to leave.

They voted to get Brexit done,

'Cos they could take no more of the Catch 22.

All they wanted was to move on.

***

Have Compassion No. 1

Have compassion for Dave.

His hometown used to be full of people just like him, and there's nothing wrong with Dave wanting to be around people who are like him, if that's what he wants. Dave doesn't hate, so he's not racist. He just wants things to be like they used to be.

So have compassion for Dave.

***

Sold Out

We've all sold out.

We're all souled out.

All full of doubt.

Be in or out,

But nowt

In between.

You're on one side or the other.

No room for middle, brother.

And so it goes, it seems.

Sold down the river.

Sold broken promise dreams.

***

How Can It Ever Be Fixed?

Brexit broke Britain.

How can it ever be fixed?

I know!

Let's call in Bob the Builder!

***

The Bumbler

We associate bumbling with lovable.

Boris knows all about that.

You can't ruffle his feathers

When he ruffles his hair,

But all I see is another fat cat.

All I see is lie after lie after lie.

That's not opinion. It's fact.

All I see is the face of Dominic Cummings

Constantly on Boris's back.

All I see is Johnson journalism,

And imitation of Trump slogans.

His moral wrestling with issues

Is as fake as a match with Hulk Hogan.

All I see is him keeping his rich pals happy

And dressing up shit as honey.

This lovable bumbler is far from a fool.

All he wants is power and money.

***

Boris Johnson Wrote These Words...

"(The EU) is a market on our doorstep, ready for further exploitation by British firms. The membership fee seems rather small for all that access. Why are we so determined to turn our back on it?"

When Boris wrote his two newspaper articles,

One pro-Brexit and one anti-Brexit,

He tried to post them in a letterbox,

But ended up shoving them in a Muslim woman's face.

***

More Little Bastards

Boris is in bed with the USA,

So there will soon be even more of Boris's bastard

children.

***

I'm Only Joking.
I Just Wish Boris Was.

I've got an oven-ready deal for you Boris.

I've lit the gas.

Just stick your head in.

***

What Was the Last Year For?

After all the blocks and debate,

And all the Cummings and goings,

And MPs leaving 'cos of hate,

We have a deal that's not even

As good as Theresa May's.

***

"Why Can't Everyone Be Like Us?"

Out of all the thousands of years in history, in all the villages, and all the towns, and all the cities, of all the countries, on all the continents, in all the world, that you could have been born into,
You think everybody should be like you and your mates down The Duck and Dive in Barnsley.

***

Establishmental

The establishment is mental.

It's off its effing head.

Politicians are psychopaths

Who take our daily bread.

All the big bankers are bonkers.

All billionaires are barmy.

And the media is crazier

Than Attila the Hun's army.

All the tycoons are cuckoo.

Advertisers foam at the mouth.

The Windsors are royal nutcases.

Whoever let them all out?

Lock 'em up in padded rooms.

Let's not get sentimental,

'Cos the elite are insane alright,

And the establishment is mental.

***

We Winced at the Prince 'Cos He Couldn't Convince

<u>Pre-interview:</u>

"Andrew, are you sure you can lie convincingly?"

"No sweat!"

<u>Post-interview:</u>

Boy, Andrew's sweating now.

***

Hey Big Pharma

The minute you walked in the joint,

I could see you were a fat cat of distinction,

A real big pharma.

Good profits. So unkind.

Say, wouldn't we like to know what's goin' on in his

mind?

So let me get right to the point,

I don't pop my pills for every doctor I see.

Hey big pharma,

Spend a lot of profits on those in poverty.

Wouldn't you like to do good, good, good?

How's about a few anti-malaria tablets for every man,

woman and child in Africa?

How's about stopping pushing pills with dangerous side-

effects on people who don't need them?

How's about providing health care as your priority?

I could show you a good time, if it was left up to me.

Let me show you how it should be!

The minute you sold your drugs for profit,

I could see you were a selfish fat cat.

A real big pharma.

Hey big pharma.

Hey big pharma.

Hey big pharma.

Spend a little time helping people.

Yes.

***

Petroleum Kisses

As petroleum kisses piss down from the clouds,

Earth-rapers and haters gun down the crowds.

As all little fishes disappear from the sea,

Fat cats talk claptrap to make more money.

As all pretty flowers divorce their bee mates,

Ministers administer more lies and hate.

As tsunamis and armies erase the past,

You prannies and fannies just sit on your arse.

***

It Used to Be Called Propaganda

The news that Fake News

Is a new thing

Is Fake News.

***

There's Always Been Fake News

I don't watch the news

To know what's going on in the world.

I watch the news

To know what the world is being told.

***

Have Compassion No. 2

Have compassion for Asim.

He was born in Putney, so all he knows is British culture.

And he gets shit from racists constantly, sometimes

kicked to the ground, simply because of the colour of

his skin and the sound of his name.

So have compassion for Asim.

***

Corbyn's End

There were no more heroes any more,

Until Corbyn called for change.

But they made sure they nailed his coffin

At the end of his brief reign.

They blamed Labour's failure

On the man and his policies,

When Brexit was the sole reason

We've been washed in the ugly blue sea.

***

Apparently, Britishness Is More Important Than Anything Else

"We want to leave the EU so we can take back complete control of the UK and make the changes we want."

"And what sorts of changes would you like to see? Perhaps good international trade relations for British businesses to be able to prosper and contribute to the national economy? Maybe free medicine, increased and cheaper public services, free broadband, new schools and hospitals, free education for all, new affordable housing, a living wage for all, and a greener way of life?"

"Well, sure. That's exactly what we want! Right, we're off to vote for Boris so we can get Brexit done."

***

Don't Look a Gift Corbyn
in the Mouth

The voters didn't believe Corbyn could deliver his gift

basket, despite it being costed and detailed.

But the voters did believe in the flimsiest Tory

manifesto there's ever been, containing lies and no

costing.

The voters all smiled every time they heard the

Tories and media use the words "magic money tree".

Another hypnosis slogan like Get Brexit Done that

everyone will repeat,

With inane aren't-I-so-witty grins on their faces.

I'm sure people said the same thing about the NHS

when it was first proposed.

Now there'd be an uproar if it was taken away.

Taking money from one pot and putting it into another

so you can help the many and not the few is nothing

whatsoever like having a - haha, wait for it, you're going

to laugh with a sneer again – "magic money tree".

But people didn't believe.

Corbyn's promises sounded too good to be true,

'Cos we're so used to living in a distrustful world of

political cons.

But couldn't you have at the very least *given him a

chance*?

***

Shake the Tree

Agadoo, doo, doo,

Shake magic money tree.

To the left. To the right.

And disguise your lies with glee.

***

Surely Remaining Neutral to Help Both Sides Is a Good Thing, Ain't It?

There's nothing at all

Wrong with Corbyn

Refusing to state his position

On Brexit in order to stay neutral.

Indeed, isn't his

Position common sense?

Better than Theresa Re-May-ner

And Boris's pretence.

But Johnson and the media

Made you believe Jeremy was shifty.

They shifted the working class to blue,

And did it real nifty.

***

See No Logic, Hear No Logic.

We've scuppered our ship.

We've covered our ears.

Smothered by the Nanny.

Loveless in our tears.

We've reshuffled the cards.

We've covered our eyes.

Soon we will discover

We won't recover from these times.

***

To Rachel Riley, Uri Geller and Others

Of course it's good to call out antisemitism,

But if you attack a man who has spent his life battling

fascism and racism,

And call him an anti-Semite,

Without a shred of evidence,

Then you're just as bad as the racists.*

***

*If you think Corbyn's handled the antisemitism within the party
badly (which I personally don't think he has), then that's one thing.
To call him an anti-Semite is quite another. Noam Chomsky agrees
with me, by the way.

Smear

Funny how all this antisemitism within the Labour party stuff only came about when Corbyn became leader.

"That's proof he's an anti-Semite then!"

No, you twat. It's proof that the smear campaign to stop socialism went into action right from the start.

***

It's Quite Simple...

Being anti-Israel does not make you an anti-Semite.

End fucking of.

***

Drip. Drip.

No media bias?

Oh yeah? What about Sky News liars

Constantly having the slogan

"The Brexit Election"

Displayed at all times?

(To mention but one example.)

This election is about one issue.

Drip. Drip.

This election is about one issue.

Drip. Drip.

Get Brexit Done.

Drip. Drip.

Get Brexit Done.

Drip. Drip.

Same tactics as advertising.

Drip. Drip.

See the slogan. Buy the product.

Drip. Drip.

See the slogan. Buy the product.

Drip. Drip.

"We're going to build a wall."

Drip. Drip.

"We're going to build a wall."

Drip. Drip.

"Get Brexit Done."

Drip. Drip.

"Get Brexit Done."

Drip. Drip.

"Starbucks two for one."

Drip. Drip.

"I'm lovin' it" (accompanied by catchy McDonald's whistle).

Drip. Drip.

Drip. Drip.

The power of suggestion.

Drip. Drip.

You drips.

***

Election Blues

Democracy doesn't work,

Because I'm in the minority,

And I know I'm right.

***

Have Compassion No. 3

Have compassion for Neil.

He grew up in a small town with small-town beliefs. And his bigoted opinions were formed by his mates who he spends all his time with, and by The Sun, which is the only news he reads. He hasn't had the opportunity to think for himself. It's just the culture he's grown up in. So have compassion for Neil.

***

Expanding Small-town Mentality

I am a working-class traitor,

Because I left my small town and I never looked back.

If things had gone another way,

Maybe my mindset would still be on the small-town

track.

***

Leavers

Of course not every leaver is a racist.

But I guarantee you every racist is a leaver.

***

Modern Albion

Hurdy-gurdy girlies

In ragged crocs

Drag across

The jagged rocks

Of zero-hour

Contract jobs.

Hurly-burly buddies

In lager shirts

Slag off all,

With spit and dirt,

And will shag all

Pieces of skirt.

Dirty surly MPs

Inbred by Eton

And the House,

Are lyin' 'n' cheatin',

'Cos history never

Stops repeating.

Pearly turdy royals

Inbred in upper

Class stolen wealth

Ensure we suffer,

'Cos history shows

We're ruled by fuckers.

Flirty shirty shift-workers,

Drifters, fisters and freaks,

Working fucking class heroes,

Muslims, Jews and Sikhs,

And all of Modern Albion,

Unite upon the rugged peaks

And sail our isle with only peace

In our hearts.

***

A Song and Dance Number

Have you seen the well-to-do,

Up and down Kremlin Avenue?

They're famous for rigging votes, so stare

At their fighter jets up in the air.

High lies and white collars.

Legal spats and lots of dollars.

Spending every ruble fine,

For a puppet-playing time.

Now, if you're blue, go where power sits…

Putin on the Ritz.

***

The Political Party

The political party

Bypasses the fun and music,

And the positive vibe where anything seems possible,

And fast-forwards to seven thirty a.m.,

When you're lying half-naked in someone else's puke,

With a cock and balls felt-tipped on your forehead.

***

Well Unfair

Their welfare is well unfair.

It will make you unwell.

They serve to scare, not to care,

As you settle down in gaol.

Their wealth air is well unfair.

You can't avoid the smell.

Well, well, wealth and welfare,

You can go to hell.

***

Employees

They used to give slaves shelter, bread and water.

Now they give slaves the minimum wage

To cover the costs of shelter, bread and water.

***

Lunatics and Slaves

When the moon waned in the house of power,

Guilt wilted like a waxwork flower.

The Sun of God shone upon the broken and brave,

While wages were invented to keep us as slaves.

From ancient times to patient rebellion,

We've been herded by the hellish hellion.

We're sold careers in the candy store,

So we'll remain slaves forever more.

Whilst they wine and dine without a care,

The slaves are too tired to whine or despair.

Guiltless, they give us our grey graves.

The lunatics who keep us as low-paid slaves.

***

A Hundred Hungered

A hundred hungered and a thousand thirsted,

And they were just a few,

Whilst you dined at fancy bistros

With a bill for a hundred or two.

Whilst you spent a fortune at Waitrose

And then threw half of the food away,

When it was found in the back of your fridge,

One day past its sell-by-date,

Another thousand thirsted,

And another hundred hungered.

Another hundred thousand died,

And another hundred thousand wondered

How the hell the food monopoly

Ended up being like this,

As the supermarkets threw their food away,

And ignored the issue with ignorant bliss.

***

Only the Rich Can Eat Healthily

If you own an orange tree,

All your oranges are free,

But if you buy fresh orange juice,

It's ten times the price of Sunny D.

***

You Can't Rhyme "Orange"

Drink orange ales

In foreign gaols.

***

Happy New Year

Hootenanny prannies whoop and cheer

When the withering witching hour appears.

One more down. Both year and beer.

Shed another lonesome tear.

A rolling die cannot be cast.

All tomorrow's parties are in the past.

Another year has gone so fast.

Another year has gone at last.

***

The Un-United Kingdom

Britain is broken.

We're all broke and not OK.

Punched in the face, KO!

Every single fucking day.

No one's offered to fix it.

The tradesmen must be on strike.

Great Britain breaks up even more

As the kingdom un-unites.

***

Independence

If you want to get rid of the United Kingdom,

Get rid of the kingdom,

Not the united.

***

Whitewolf's Prediction

First came independence for the countries.

Then came independence for the counties.

Then came independence for the boroughs.

Then came independence for the cities,

Followed by the towns and the villages.

Then came independence for each road.

Then came independence for each house,

Followed by independence for each room.

Now everyone's at war.

***

Have Compassion No. 4

Have compassion for Ayesha.

She spent years being ravaged by war, followed by years in a slum of a refugee camp, and then months of dangerously crossing borders in the back of refrigerated trucks just to get to Britain and escape the horrors she's known all her life. And now she gets spat upon in the street and told to "go home" just because she wasn't born in Britain.

So have compassion for Ayesha.

***

Democracy Doesn't Work

Democracy doesn't work,

When we're given little choice.

Democracy doesn't work,

When the voters believe lies.

Democracy doesn't work,

When the most-funded campaign wins.

Democracy doesn't work,

When the facts are filtered through spin.

Democracy doesn't work,

When there is no party that reflects my beliefs.

Democracy doesn't work,

When it supports a system of financial thieves.

Democracy doesn't work,

When it only serves the Kafkapitalist system.

Democracy doesn't work,

When there isn't any empathy, love or wisdom.

***

The Dumb Drum

I'm still dumbfounded

To find the dumb everywhere.

I'm still flabbergasted

At the tat they watch and wear

And read and buy,

And chat about.

Stupidity is common.

Of that I have no doubt.

But it's not their fault.

They are dumbed down.

They're dumped upon

From higher ground.

Educate Rita

And you might find,

People start

To change their minds.

But as for now,

It's bang the dumb drum.

The people will love it.

Look out! Here they come!

***

Empathy Versus Selfishness

If everyone voted to help everyone else,

Rather than themselves,

And their personal situations,

The political landscape

Would look very different.

***

Represent the People

All wannabe-MPs from privileged backgrounds should be forced to work in Amazon warehouses on zero-hour contracts for three years, while having no other source of income, before they are allowed to become MPs.

Yes, a degree in economics is certainly handy for running parliament.
But experiencing what it's like to work like a bastard and still be in dire poverty is even more important.

***

Albion Albinos

Albion albinos

Don't want cappuccinos

Or Italian Pacinos

Or Mexican burritos

Or Cuban mojitos.

But Albion albinos

Love eating Doritos,

'Cos white America's alright.

***

Have Compassion No. 5

Have compassion for Theresa.

After three years of receiving shit, she's had to sit in silence while she watched Boris be crowned in glory and get a deal that's worse than her own, as she wonders why the hell she had to step down, and what the point of the last year was.

So have compassion for Theresa.

***

You've Got to Be
a Leaver or a Remainer

I'm against the EU,

And I'm against the UK,

'Cos it's the political system

I want to see change.

I imagine like Lennon,

That there's no countries.

No borders to divide us.

No minister numpties.

I want to see an end to division.

I want to see financial equality.

I want a system that works for all.

Not this charade game monopoly.

There are so many bigger issues

Than reclaiming Britishness as an idea.

But they distract us and divide us,

And sedate us with TV and beer,

So we'll never rise against

The corrupt and unjust system.

I say burn all of our flags

And start again with wisdom.

***

Modern Tribes

Right versus Left.

Capitalist versus Socialist.

Conservative versus Labour.

Remainer versus Leaver.

North versus South.

Pro-immigration versus Anti-immigration.

The Sun reader versus The Guardian reader.

Stop getting distracted with irrelevant divisions.

There's only one division we need to fight:

The division between the rich and the poor.

But sure,

If you'd rather bury your heads in the sand and focus more

On the divisions listed above, then that's up to you I guess.

But it's the reason financial equality is never achieved.

***

Dead Cats and Deals

Dead cats and deals.

Setbacks and bills.

Send back all the immigrants

And asylum innocents,

Goes the boring Bexitcast spiel.

Headlines and deadlines,

Breadlines and bedtimes,

Make us wallow in blood and swill.

We're dead pigs

Smoking cigs.

Not felines with cigars.

We're trained like dogs,

Mimic groundhogs,

In broken deadbeat bars.

Headlines and deadlines.

Breadlines and dead times.

Brexit setbacks and bills.

It's all dead cats and deals.

85

***

The Side of Divide

I don't care about Left. I don't care about Right.

I will never be on the side of Divide.

I care about hate and I care about love.

All other sides can be shoved

Up your arse. Forget the division.

Focus on breaking out of the prison,

Together. United, we'll win.

Let the Age of Empathy begin.

What a world we would discover!

But you keep fighting one another.

Straight versus gay. White versus black.

Male versus nonbinary. Beer versus crack.

Muslim versus Christian. Left versus Right.

I will never be on the side of Divide.

Unity's the answer. Stop dividing.

Only one thing is worth fighting:

Hate.

***

You Can Count on Counter Culture

You can't count on the cunts,

But you can count on counter culture.

We don't move like counters

Or behave like fat cat vultures.

We don't have grand titles like Viscount.

We don't have counties we own in our names.

We don't have countless dollars to burn.

We don't count profits made from stock gains.

But we count our lucky blessings,

As we count down the hours and days.

We don't discount the idea of peace,

And we can count on each other always.

****

Free of Flags

When we are free of all flags,

We will evolve with love.

When we discard our hardships,

We'll sail the oceans above.

When we break from self-made chains,

We will all be changed.

When there's no place for prejudice,

We will not be estranged.

When we divorce division,

We will rise to new states of being.

It all begins with freeing ourselves from flags

And the power systems we believe in.

***

OTHER BOOKS BY HARRY WHITEWOLF

POETRY

New Beat Newbie

Two Beat Newbie

Rhyme and Rebellion

Underdogs Unite

Primordial Youth - The Early Poems: '96 - '99

Propaganda Monkeys - Twenty Poems
from My Twenties: 1996 - 2006

Indie Poet - Thirty Poems from My Thirties: 2006 - 2016

Matrix Visions

TRUE TRAVEL TALES

Route Number 11: Argentina, Angels & Alcohol

The Road to Purification: Hustlers, Hassles & Hash

FICTION

Reejecttllon – A Number Two

(A collaboration with Daniel Clausen)

THE ANTI-AUSTERITY ANTHOLOGY

Foreword by journalist and activist **Steve Topple**

Edited by **Rupert Dreyfus**, **Harry Whitewolf** & **Mike Robbins**

All proceeds from this book will be donated to

food bank charities

This powerful collection of short stories, poems and essays is brought to you by some of the indie author scene's most talented and radical writers. Thoughtful, funny, tragic, angry, and filled with hope, each contributor uses their craft to speak out against the damning, ideologically-driven measures that are inflicted upon society.

The time for change is now.

WWW.HARRYWHITEWOLF.COM